TOULOUSE-LAUTREC

TOULOUSE-LAUTREC

PERE GIMFERRER

RIZZOLI
NEW YORK

First published in the United States of America in 1990 by

RIZZOLI INTERNATIONAL PUBLICATIONS, INC.
300 Park Avenue South, New York, NY 10010

© *1990 Ediciones Polígrafa, S. A.*
Translated by Angela Patricia Hall

LC 90-52970
ISBN 0-8478-1276-6

Color separations by Reprocolor Llovet, S. A., Barcelona
Printed and bound by La Polígrafa, S. A.
Parets del Vallès (Barcelona)
Dep. Leg. B. 29.712 - 1990 (Printed in Spain)

LAUTREC: PAINTED IMAGES

The style of Toulouse-Lautrec took shape very early. Not only its characteristics but also the pertinent areas of interest had been perfectly established by the time the artist was twenty years old; when he was twenty-two, a work such as *Ballet Scene* in the Thielska Galleriet Stockholm — not so well known as it should be, since it is to be found in a museum which owes its fame to the excellent collection of Scandinavian paintings contained there — already offered all the characteristics that would define the artist, as regards not only drawing, color and how he dealt with space, but also the motifs on which he centered his art. It is necessary here to delimit two sets of problems. On the one hand, the Lautrec whom we here find so well-formed almost from the beginning did not fundamentally change his style until the last two years of his life; on the other, the reason why his work varied during these last two years has not been clarified, and neither is there complete agreement among critics as to the value and significance of several works from this last period. Both questions will therefore be examined separately.

The style and the world of Toulouse-Lautrec, as they were formed from the mid eighteen-eighties up until 1898, are enough to convert his name into a crucial one within modern artistic currents; his work most definitely marks a stage in the evolution of lithographic techniques, but also, by virtue of his drawings and paintings, he can be situated amongst the great innovators who laid the foundations for the contemporary plastic arts. As no one can deny his achievements here, it would be better not to pretend that we are ignorant of the fact that the more characteristic work of Lautrec has lent itself to two sorts of errors. Firstly, the extraordinarily flagrant scenes of the brothel, theater, café and music hall, with their extremely high documentary value and frankness, that was frequently novel in the history of art and which singularized them, have made some people think of Lautrec above all as the painter of an era. Furthermore, this era is also extraordinarily spectacular: it is the start of the *belle époque*, that is not the period when the main action of Proust's novel cycle took place, but the period immediately prior to it which corresponds, in this aforementioned cycle, to the more or less juvenile loves of the character Charles Swann. Moreover, there is the basic difference that Lautrec was alien to the aristocratic salons — to which, given his lineage, he could have had easy access — which constituted the nucleus of magnetization for Proust, and interested Lautrec rather, in areas which Proust merely touched upon and only then in their homosexual variants: the worlds of entertainment and of prostitution.

In the form in which Lautrec portrays them — so true and at the same time so fascinating, like Goya or Daumier each in his own way — such ambits remain completely closed and sealed for ever within the frontiers of a specific time: they belong to Maupassant's Paris, of whose visual existence we have no documents (not even daguerreotypes or photographs) of greater relevance or more effective veracity. It is impossible to avoid the attraction of such things, but we would be doing Lautrec less than justice if we appreciated him only for these. No one thinks to appreciate Velázquez (to mention an artist whom Lautrec admired) merely because of the documentary value of his work in respect to life in the court of Philip IV. Furthermore, in this case the said life remains very distant from our daily experience and it immediately comes to mind that, however good a courtesan Velázquez might have been, his artistic concerns were of another order. On the other hand, the world which Lautrec created is situated in the immediate genealogy of our society and it is evident that the artistic treatment here reflects the artist's personal fascination for, or real dependence on, the world he depicts in his work.

However, it is evident that Lautrec has the right for his works to be contemplated in the same way as those of Velázquez: documents of the era, certainly, but first of all as an independent art. Of course, it would be impossible to disguise the fact that the visual aspects of their respective periods, maintained by Velázquez and Lautrec, are of very different natures. Lautrec particularly eludes the problems of space with which Velázquez was deeply concerned and Lautrec's striving for documentary realism and his desire to obtain a visual impact through the unusual and striking combination of forms observed in daily life are preoccupations and designs that, in the form in which he presents them, could only be found in a painter from the end of the nineteenth century, as in any previous period they would have been considered inappropriate to the idea of artistic decorum, which was not merely aesthetic but above all concerned with the question of morals. But while probably the first artist to show such preoccupations, Lautrec was far from being the last: to mention only one exemplary case, a few years after the death of Lautrec the young Picasso was in his own way expressing the same concerns.

The temptation therefore having been dispelled or rejected (and it is more treacherously widespread than is usually believed) to appreciate Lautrec for the taste of the period in his work, there exists still another stumbling block: the question that, as the essential characteristic of this art is the immediate capture of the human gesture in a precise social environment, could this then be a case not of serious art but of an art nearer to caricature, that is, very innovative and attractive, but inextricably linked to a lesser genre? Lautrec ridiculed the pictorial symbolism of Puvis de Chavannes; should we therefore infer from this that in his painting he renounced such profound ambitions as those which motivated Puvis de Chavannes? It is true that the art of Lautrec is almost aggressively anti-intellectual, based on an expansive physical and sensory vitality; but it is, beyond doubt, the aspiration towards serious art that held our artist firmly on course.

The problem was suitably posed by Douglas Cooper when he wrote: "It was principally Lautrec's ability to observe human beings without indulging in physical, moral, or social criticism which saved his work from falling into caricature or becoming mere illustration — risks which Degas never ran — and this is an essential part of his greatness." Indeed, if we observe one of Lautrec's most important works, *In the Salon of the Rue des Moulins* (1894), an immediate iconic antecedent to Picasso's *Les Demoiselles d'Avignon*, it is possible to see at once that Lautrec's sights were set very high: he did not then criticize Puvis de Chavannes because the latter was ambitious, but rather because it seemed to him that Chavannes conformed to a substitute for true artistic ambition, to an imitation of past greatness, instead of aspiring to the

7

Puvis de Chavannes: *The Sacred Grove*. 1884.
Mural on canvas, 180¾ × 55½ in. (4.59 × 1.41 m). Musée de Lyon.

The Sacred Grove. Winter of 1884. (Parody of the panel exhibited by Puvis de Chavannes in the 1884 Salon.)
67 × 145¼ in. (170 × 369 cm). Henry Pearlman Col., New York.

greatness of today, which by definition would be the truly timeless greatness for observers of the future.

In effect, the greatness which Puvis de Chavannes was able to achieve was in the best of cases (and there is reason why today his works deserve more esteem on our part than they did on Lautrec's part at the time) the greatness of an echo, reflection, evocation or semblance of the candid ecstasy of medieval art. The greatness of a painting such as *In the Salon of the Rue des Moulins* is, however, on the same level of greatness as *Les Demoiselles d'Avignon*: a new and specific form of beauty which, whatever its links may be to tradition, believes above all in modernity. This painting is beautiful, not because it is similar to other beautiful paintings from the past, but because it proposes another form of unknown beauty, because it discovers beauty where no one had looked for nor managed to see it before; in fact it *does* come to resemble other older beautiful paintings, but only to the extent in which we, finally accustomed to its peculiar formulation of beauty, are able to reduce the world which surrounds the artist, as he himself did, to pure visual and chromatic enunciation. In this sense, one beautiful painting looks much like another, and one form of beauty is worth the same as another; but when the world is reduced to visual forms and to chromaticism it means appealing to the highest instances of artistic perception, to the most uncompromising feature of painting. Not the imitation of the maestros, nor exactly of reality, but rather — and let us not be afraid of the words — the ideal model of beauty, latent beneath the surface of the world of the senses, to which all artists since antiquity have referred. In this sense, only those who truly know how to be classical will know how to be modern: that Lautrec, and later Picasso, should admire Ingres, is by no means a fortuitous occurrence.

As we have already said, from 1898, that is to say during the last two years of his life, Lautrec's painting was very different from his previous work: the flowing outlines, inspired by the engravings of the Japanese maestros, are replaced by a sensual, doughy and compact accumulation of pictorial material. We have already indicated that different opinions exist as to the causes of this abrupt change (which some attribute to hitherto unclarified aesthetic causes and others to a necessary adaptation to the limitations imposed by the shaky wrist of an alcoholic) and even concerning its value; and there is no question that several masterpieces exist amongst the canvases from these years, but others have as many admirers as detractors. In any case, it is evident that the brevity of the period makes any judgment hypothetical and irremediably provisional. Even so, we must stop and consider it.

It is no coincidence that Picasso's name has already been mentioned several times, because here we have arrived at the Gordian knot of a great debate. When Lautrec died, Picasso was twenty years old. The poet Jaime Gil de Biedma, an illustrious visitor to the Albi Museum, who was a long way from being an art critic, but who possessed exceptional intellectual qualities, formed the following observation of Lautrec: "It is curious to observe what Picasso became thanks to him, and one asks if there would have been room for this development if Lautrec had not died at 37 years of age, because the impression that the whole of the Albi collection creates is that of a man with as exceptionally creative gifts as those of Picasso and with as extraordinarily an instinctive intelligence as his." The observation is completely truthful — as much concerning Lautrec's role as forerunner to Picasso, as regarding the vitality and creative energy of the painter from Albi — even though the development of Lautrec's work in his last years leads to the suspicion that his artistic career would certainly have followed unforeseen routes, sufficiently different from those which at the end of the day Picasso followed clearly revealing the generation gap which separated them. It is impossible to know what path Lautrec would have taken had he lived longer; but the predominance of the pictorial material over outline in the works of his final years situate his experiences of this period in territories less akin to those which Picasso was to explore than what can be inferred from his previous production. Problems of space, always central in Picasso, were eluded — or at least elided, sidestepped by means of a visual resolution similar to bas-relief, as Cooper indicates — in the more characteristic Lautrecs; however, in the last years of his life Lautrec hardly needed to elude them, because his treatment of the pictorial material acquired much more importance than any other factor.

We inevitably get the impression that any controversy with respect to these final paintings is destined to remain within the limits of the particular tastes of each individual, not exactly with regard to those works on which there exists a generalized critical accord, such as *The Reticent One or "Au Rat Mort* or *La Coutourière (Louise Blouet d'Enguin)*, whose beauty — disturbing in the first case, sensually calm and serene in the second — does not ask for special elucidation, but with regard to the creations which have awoken greater perplexities, the most important and characteristic of which is the last great undertaking by Toulouse-Lautrec: *An Examination in the Faculty of Medicine in the University of Paris* (1901). By virtue of its involuntarily testamentary character, and because it carries to an extraordinary degree the interrogations and paradoxes of the artist's final period, it is worth our while to briefly examine it here.

The first thing which calls our attention in the scene depicted is a somber monumentality. In describing it, it is hard to conceive a qualifying epithet other than that of expressionist, without this signifying that I would abusively assign the work to a tendency which has its precise place in the historiography of art. It is evident that both the threatening masses of color and form of the members of the tribunal and, particulary, the moroseness and the ominous look of the personage situated more to the right of the spectator, introduce a different vision to the one we usually admire in Lautrec who, being a realist painter, is always a painter who stylizes realism and, as I said earlier, refers what is real to iconic facts.

But now this enterprise began to follow new paths: not only did Lautrec concentrate on pictorial materiality, on its thickness and density, but he disturbingly introduced the element which, of all the painting, most powerfully attracts the attention of we the observers, even supposing that we do not notice this at first, that is, that we are not capable of rationalizing it, since without doubt our instinctive perception would have registered it right from the start. I am referring, of course, to the clearly disproportionate size of the hands of this member of the tribunal which, by virtue of their singularity and of their position on the canvas, become the observer's main point of attention, highlighted also by the fact that the right hand holds a pen and seems to be in the act of writing — no doubt an academic assessment — in an overly laborious way, with special difficulty, as though he were hindered not only by the gigantic deformity of his constitution, but also by a certain insidious contagion from the weight of the mass of paint which Lautrec has applied to represent the scene.

Very varied value judgments have been given, regarding not only the artistic merit of this work, but also its very *raison d'être*. For some — Cooper amongst them — it is a sign of the physical and spiritual decline of the artist, a retrospective tribute to the ten years of exceptional creativity which preceded Toulouse-Lautrec's hospitalization. Others, however, see in this painting, more markedly even than in others, the threshold of a new period whose possibilities were never explored to the full due to the premature death of the painter. Strictly speaking neither hypothesis can be discounted. That his physical condition and state of mind had made Lautrec take a specific path does not mean that this path was necessarily alien to his temperament; it might not be a symptom of decline but, quite the opposite, a way of avoiding decline by adjusting his style to the possibilities available to him at that moment. In the same way that in the past he avoided frontally tackling problems of space by resorting to a technique which bordered on bas-relief, he was now able to concentrate more on pictorial matter than on outline and, if formerly he had been tempted by the fine lines of the Japanese masters, he could now stylize reality by means of its deformation through the aforesaid matter.

As for the rest, the extreme severity of the scene and its disturbing character of visionary hallucination are completely appropriate to the evolution of Lautrec's world view. Therefore, what do we see here, exactly? The same as in any other of Lautrec's work from the past: a scene of everyday life which is transfigured by being the object of artistic representation. Although the technique used is very different, the artistic and moral attitude of Lautrec before the examining board of the Paris Faculty of Medicine at bottom is no different, for example, from that which he adopted concerning the personage with the hat and mustache situated on the right in the painting *In the Moulin de la Galette* (1889), which is at present in the Art Institute in Chicago. In effect, the artistic operations carried out are of a similar nature in both cases, even though technically they are very dissimilar: it is a case of converting the visual factor that most characterizes a personage into a compositional element, to change the personage into an ideogram of himself.

Even the innermost displeasure that we cannot help but feel when contemplating the music hall environment, in which we detect behind the splendor the livid death masks the personages wear, is at bottom a sensation akin to the one which assails us on contemplating this tribunal, evoking atavistic terrors and insecurities much more profound than the trivial enigma of an academic assessment. Like all great artists, at all moments in his work Lautrec alludes to the major uncertainties and anxieties of the human being and, in their artistic representation, expresses the essential enigma of our condition. The extent to which in one way or another the said representation departs from conformity to classical canons and flows along hitherto unexplored channels, new to art, determines how far it is able to share the profound nature of what is represented.

Having thus postulated the fundamental unity of the art of Lautrec, is it perhaps permissible for us now to examine, beyond the stylistic problem of the break in his last period, two essential characteristics of his work: on the one hand, the bifurcation between scenes of the world of the stage and pleasure in Paris, and scenes of daily life, and on the other, the nature common to of all of them as "painted images." I hasten to make clear that I give these last two words the same significance as Giorgio de Chirico gave them when he indicated that until 1919 "in the museums of Italy, France and Germany I had contemplated the paintings of the maestros and had always seen them as everyone sees them; that is to say, as *painted images.*" In the meaning of Giorgio de Chirico, the perception of "painted images" comes prior to the perception of the same work as "great painting," and one does not always reach this last stage.

Without the necessity of following the particular strategy of Chirico, it is possible to use this term to describe, or at least to attempt to describe, both the uniqueness of the work of Lautrec and the fact that the strange fascination it exercises does not always, due to the particular characteristics which are to be found there, give way to the appreciation of the singularity of his aesthetic experience, to the point where it can be said that for many observers the beauty of his creations belongs — as has already been said — either to the sphere of the document of the period, or else to the immanent sphere of ineffable plastic creation; as if at bottom, in the form of a pure phenomenal occurrence, it resists any explanation other than its strict and absolute artistic presence.

Precisely because they are essentially complementary, these two interpretations seem to be mutually exclusive. If something neither requires nor admits explanation apart from its visual existence, how can we conform simply to describing it as a document of the period? And, in any case, while these scenes of the brothel or music hall may attract us in this last sense, what about the equally great attraction of so many scenes of life in the provinces or of daily life alien to pleasure and the world of entertainment, and finally of the frightening tribunal of the Medical Faculty? What can we say about the poignant portraits of family and friends?; what of the elusive poetry of *La Coutourière*? It as well to point out that such representations, which at first glance seem to attract us as "painted images," in truth draw us in the deeper, lasting, even archetypal way of "great painting."

Few artists have equaled Lautrec in his faith in the phenomenal veracity of the surrounding world and in the capacity of the human eye to apprehend it. Though his images may in themselves be of intimate and withdrawn modesty or on many occasions of undeniable sordidness, it is precisely from this faith that the deep sense of human dignity that moves us in his work is derived. For example, Lautrec is, or frequently borders on being, a painter of sexual activity, but he is not really a painter of sensuality (as were, each in his own way, Rubens, Titian, Fragonard and Renoir). No: what characterizes Lautrec is that for him sexual activity does not belong to a different territory from that of any other type of activity contained within human experience as a whole. Sexuality is not for him an occupation of the realms of the erotic, a ritual that imitates atavistic beliefs and traditions, or a refinedly clandestine act confined to the boudoir; quite the opposite, it is another element of the greatness or helplessness of our daily life. It therefore follows that the type of seduction which the two thematically divided sectors of his work wield over us is at bottom, regarding what really matters, wholly analogous, since it is a seduction of "great painting," not merely of "painted images."

The white dress, the pallid face, the red hair and green eyes of the patroness of the brothel in *In the Salon of the Rue des Moulins*, overpowering like a gargoyle or a macabre mask, essentially enclose the same type of experience as the face of the Countess of Toulouse-Lautrec in the salon of Malromé, painted seven years earlier in 1887. There is nothing disrespectful here on the part of Lautrec: in these severe and terrible images of women faced

Lautrec and Métivet (painter and humorist).

The Moorish room in the Rues des Moulins.

with their own aging process and ultimately their own death, the look of the artist cannot but instinctively recognize the fraternity of the human being, lost in visible space, alone with his destiny. The essential compassion of Lautrec, despite his acute gift for satirical observation, rests precisely on the deep perception he shows of what everyone has in common and, in consequence, on his refusal to classify people into plastic hierarchies: they are visual facts in the same way that they are human creatures, that is, the same before the eyes of the painter as before the common destiny that existence prepares.

Any of Lautrec's works, from the most famous to the less well known, respond from this basic stance. It is enough to examine one, almost at random, which is neither thoroughly unknown nor of the most famous: the oil portrait of Gabriel Tapié de Céleyran, painted in 1894. The subject — Lautrec's cousin, and incidentally the person being examined in the aforementioned Medical Faculty painting — appears standing in one of the corridors of the Comédie Française with a top hat and a walking stick. At first glance, we would say the attractiveness of the canvas resides above all in its intelligent composition and in its use of color. The vivid reddish-orange color of the floor, which we find echoed in the identical tone of the curtain which we see through the opening in the top left hand margin of the canvas, together with the slope of the angle of vision, which seems to obliquely reveal the personage — an unusual pictorial composition which anticipates a perspective that was to emerge with the expressionist cinema and which Orson Welles was to use regularly: filming from below with a tilted camera — at first glance and by virtue of their striking nature seem to be the elements that define the aesthetic success of the work. But very soon the observer's eye captures in the background the green dress and red hair of the feminine figure standing on the threshold with her back to us; and, at the level of this figure's shoulder, in a sort of halo produced by the effect of the illumination of the theatre, which creates an atmosphere of pure unreality, we see appear, visually imprisoned or encased between the shoulder covered in green cloth with black lacing and the shoulder covered with the black cloth of the evening suit of Gabriel Tapié, a nightmarish face, similar to those which can be seen in Goya's black paintings or *Caprichos*: a type of ill-fated personification of the night life of Paris.

Could the conspiracy of red, green and black, with the background of this unnerving face, situate this work in the realm of oneiric allegory, similar to certain poetic visions Baudelaire had of the big city? It is true that this possibility exists, and is an undeniable part of the impact of the work. But if we look at what truly forms the center of the piece — that is, the figure of Gabriel Tapié de Céleyran — soon we observe that neither what we see to the back of the personage nor the reddish frame or support against which he is set is as important as his attitude. What he is doing could not be simpler or more trivial: he is merely smoking pensively, during an interval, oblivious to his surroundings, to all the human figures, however striking they may be, and to the spark thrown out by the reddish colour which bathes, surrounds and in a way sustains the scene. We find Gabriel Tapié alone with himself as though he were in the countryside around Albi; as alone, to be sure, as he will finally be before the awesome tribunal of the Medical Faculty of the University of Paris; as alone as we ourselves are, with our being in the world. More than resignation or indifference, in his stance there is awareness of his own condition, and this awareness is imminent in his pictorial existence: it derives from his posture, certainly, but also from the contrast, deliberate as well as highly natural, between this posture and the phantasmagoria of the background and the reddish splendor of the floor and the curtain. What Lautrec paints here, with the loneliness of man, is man'shis fundamental dignity.

The profound modernity of Lautrec resides here, more than in any other aspect. The poetry of the past spoke of gods and heroes; with Baudelaire and later with Rimbaud it goes on to talk of men in contemporary society, and there sometimes glimpses new, disturbing myths which emblematically allude the world in which the poet lives. In the same way, Lautrec — as before him Velázquez or Goya, and a little later Picasso — did not concern himself with fabulous gigantomachies and scenography, in the way that the (otherwise so often admirable) mannerist painters did. If he depicted visible reality as an artistic fact, if the seduction of his painted images — so bold and of an exemplary inventiveness and vitality — is the seduction of great painting, then no matter the nature of what is expressed, however exotic or bizarre it may be, the ultimate objective of Lautrec's work is the rediscovering of the human gesture in its most naked truth, that custom veiled with the conventional forms of academic representation, once operational, but later without life in the time of Lautrec.

So Lautrec, like Rimbaud, becomes a clairvoyant. His profound realist vocation forces him to this: only by seeing things in a radically new way could he be sure that he would truly see them and make others see them too. The essence of his art would later be that of contemporary art and the roots of the avant-garde: the criticism of perception, implicit in the criticism of representation, directed towards the awakening of the true human condition.

PERE GIMFERRER
Real Academia Española, Madrid

BIOGRAPHY

1864

On the night of November 24, Henri Marie Raymond de Toulouse-Lautrec Monfa is born in the small palace of Albi, the son of Count Alphonse Charles de Toulouse-Lautrec Monfa and his cousin Adèle Marquette Tapié de Céleyran. The newly born child is given the name Henri in honor of the legitimate heir to the French throne, Henri, Duke of Bordeaux and Count of Chambord. Although the relationship with the sovereign counts of Toulouse-Lautrec has not been established with all certainty, the Toulouse-Lautrec Monfa are one of the great families of the southeast. Related to the Tapié de Céleyran family, the numerous matrimonies which had taken place between the two families had created complicated ties. The father, grandparents, uncles and aunts and the grandmother of the last born are, every one of them, talented amateur painters.

1867

On August 28 a second son is born and given the name Richard in memory of Richard of England, whose sister had married a Lautrec.

1868

The infant Richard dies in Loury, Sologne, where the Count of Toulouse-Lautrec possesses hunting reserves. The Count and Countess separate by mutual agreement. Henri is educated in the southeast, in the castles of Bosc and of Céleyran. He studies in the home of Dom Peyre, who teaches him Latin and Greek, and with Armandine d'Alichoux de Sénègue, who gives him classes in general culture.

1872

The family move to Paris and instal themselves in the Hôtel Perey, in the Rue Boissy d'Anglas in the Cité du Retiro, and later in Neuilly. Henri enters the Lycée Fontanes (today Condorcet). He meets students who are to become lifelong friends: Louis Pascal and Murice Joyant. Henri draws all he sees in his school exercise books.

1874

He returns to Albi with his mother. He studies with a private tutor. Delicate in health, he has to undergo a course of treatment in Amélie-Les-Bains.

1878

On May 30 he falls off a chair and is so unlucky as to break his leg.

1879

In August, whilst walking with his mother in Barèges, he slips and falls into a hole, fracturing his right femur. The bone never properly knits and his legs stop growing. This is not in fact purely an accident but the consequence of a malformation due to inbreeding.

1880

He goes on to convalesce in Nice, Albi and Céleyran without interrupting his studies.

1881

In Paris, where his family has returned, he sits his Baccalaureate exam and fails. He spends the summer in Nice. He writes his travel impressions in the *Cahier de Zigzags*, a short manuscript illustrated with a large number of drawings, which he dedicates to his cousin Madeleine Tapié de Céleyran. After a period of treatment in Lamalou-les-Bains he returns to Albi. Étienne Devisme writes the novel *Cocotte*, for which Lautrec does the illustrations. He had met Devisme in Barèges in 1879. He passes his Baccalaureate in Toulouse in November and returns to Paris where he presents his drawings to the painter René Princeteau, a friend of his father's.

1882

He spends the winter in Albi and Céleyran. In March he works in Princeteau's studio in the Faubourg Saint-Honoré in Paris. He meets Forain, a satirical artist and friend of his father's, and the Irish painter John Lewis Brown. His friend Henri Rachou, also a painter, recommends him to Bonnat and he enters the studio of the "beloved maestro." Bonnat does not like Lautrec's work and the relationship between maestro and student becomes strained. Bonnat closes his studio at the end of the year.

1883

With other ex-pupils of Bonnat he presents himself at the studio of Fernand Cormon, called "Le Père la Rotule," a far more liberal person than Bonnat. The group consists of Émile Bernard, Anquetin, Laval, Fauché, Gauzi and Grenier.

1884

He and Grenier move into number 19 bis, Rue Fontaine, where Degas resides and from whom he seeks advice. Later he moves into Henri Rachou's house, at number 22 Rue Ganneron, having previously rented a studio in Rue Tourlaque. He takes part in a group exhibition in Pau. He goes to paint in the Jardin du Père Forest, between Rue Caulaincourt and Boulevard de Clichy.

1885

Aristide Bruant opens his cabaret "Le Mirliton," where Lautrec will show his works. He has a short-lived and tumultuous relationship with Suzanne Valadon, whose talent Lautrec had discovered.

1886

He spends the summer in Malromé, near the Bassin du Arcachon, in Bordelais, where his mother had bought a castle. He does humoristic drawings for the newspapers, meets Van Gogh and exhibits at the Salon des Arts Incohérents under the name of Tolau-Segroeg.

1887

He takes part in a group exhibition in Toulouse, in which his works appear signed under the pseudonym of Treclau, an anagram of Lautrec. He stays in the house of his friend, Doctor Bourges, in the Rue Fontaine; he does a pastel color portrait of Van Gogh and paints several interiors of the Moulin Rouge.

1888

By invitation from Octave Maux, he takes part in the XX of Brussels exhibition. The critics look favorably on the eleven works he presents. The only ones to show hostility are Ensor and Signac. Théo van Gogh, brother of Vincent, who works at the Boussod et Valadon gallery, takes several of his canvases into deposit.

1889

Lautrec exhibits at the Salon des Indépendants and at the Cercle Volney, both in Paris. He remains in Les Indépendants until 1894. He visits the Universal Exhibition and spends the summer in Arcachon, where he wins several regattas. He exhibits once again at the Salon des Arts Incohérents. Théo van Gogh buys several canvases for the Goupil Gallery. The inauguration of the Moulin Rouge. At the entrance Lautrec exhibits the canvas *At the Circus Fernando: the Amazon*.

1890

The banquet of the XX exhibition in Brussels, where he challenges the painter Henri de Groux to a duel for criticizing the works of Van Gogh. The duel never takes place. Van Gogh commits suicide. Lautrec spends the summer in Provence. Théo van Gogh falls ill, leaves the Goupil Gallery, and his friend Joyant takes over as manager. Oller, the manager of the Moulin Rouge, buys *In the Moulin Rouge: the Dance* and hangs it in the bar of his establishment. Lautrec meets Jane Avril and for a time moves into a brothel in the Rue des Moulins, where he has a love affair with Blanche, one of the prostitutes.

1891

His cousin Gabriel Tapié de Celeyran goes to Paris to finish his medical studies and introduces Lautrec to the hospital environment. Lautrec paints Doctor Péan operating. Favourable criticism of an exhibition held in a venue opened by Le Barc de Boutteville, who would later manage a gallery. Lautrec produces his first lithographic poster for the Moulin Rouge and becomes interested in Japanese art, copying designs by Hokusai, Utamaro, Kyonaga and Harunobu.

1892

Exhibition of the XX, later in the Cercle Volney and the Le Barc de Boutteville gallery, where it is highly successful.

1893

He meets Yvette Guilbert. Joyant organizes an exhibition for him at the Boussod et Valadon Gallery. The reviews are favorable. He is invited to show his paintings in Brussels and Antwerp. As a result of the marriage of Doctor Bourges, Lautrec leaves the Rue Fontaine and moves into the house his mother has rented in Rue de Douai, to be near her son and to watch over him. He decorates the salon of an elegant brothel in the Rue d'Ambroise, at the request of the manageress, Blanche d'Egmont. He frequents Whistler's studio and makes prints for the Estampes Originales publishing house and for the music publisher Georges Ondet.

He exhibits twelve lithographs at the V exhibition of painter-engravers.

1894

He participates in the Salon de la Libre Esthétique and in the Centre de l'Art Nouveau in Brussels. As in other years, he goes to London to exhibit his posters in the Royal Aquarium. He meets Oscar Wilde and comes across Whistler, whom he invites to a great supper at the Savoy. In Toulouse, in May, an exhibition of avant-garde painters is organized by *La Dépêche*, an important newspaper from the southeast. He meets the Natansons, the proprietors of *La Revue Blanche*, Tristan Bernard, Romain Coolus and Félix Fénéon. His album of lithographs dedicated to Yvette Guilbert obtains excellent reviews. He moves to the brothel in the Rue des Moulins, where he executes a series of portraits of prostitutes and one of his most important works, entitled *In the Salon of the Rue des Moulins*.

1895

Having left the Moulin Rouge, La Goulue requests him to decorate the shanty she has just bought in the Foire du Trône. He takes part in several group exhibitions. He goes often to the theatre and does the scenery for the play by Barrucaud, *Chariot de terre cuite*, and a great many lithographs on the same subject. He frequents the Théâtre des Variétés, where Marcelle Lender sings and dances in Hervé's operetta *Chilpéric*. The German magazine, *Pan* publishes one of this lithographs in eight colors, which constitutes a great event at the time. The same year, in the Natansons' house on the Avenue du Bois, he disguises himself as a barman during a reception and, even though he himself does not drink, he prepares formidable cocktails which the guests cannot resist.

1896

Exhibition in the Goupil Gallery in the Rue Forest. Isaac de Camondo acquires a major canvas. On the other hand he refuses to sell a painting to the king of Serbia, whom he describes as "a dealer in pigs." He does a series of lithographs titled *Elles*, for the publisher Gustave Pellet in remembrance of his stays in brothels. The album is not successful. Tristan Bernard introduces him to the world of sport, especially to the cycle track. Lautrec becomes an enthusiast of this sport, which he cannot practice, and he designs the famous poster for Simpson bicycle chains. To travel to the southeast in the summer, he goes to Le Havre and boards the *Chili*, where he meets a female passenger who never speaks to him, and he decides to follow her to Dakar. His friend Guibert, who is accompanying him on the trip, prevents him from carrying out his plan.

1897

He leaves his studio in Rue Tourlaque and moves to Rue Frochot, leaving behind eighty-seven paintings, most of which will be destroyed by the next tenant. He goes on trips to the bay of La Somme and Holland, spending his holidays with the Natansons on their estate in Villeneuve-sur-Yonne. His first crisis of delirium tremens; he fires at imaginary spiders with a pistol. He hardly paints, but designs theatre programs and does a lithograph for Vollard.

1898

The English publisher Sanders asks him to do a series of lithographs on Yvette Guilbert. The exhibition is organized by Joyant in the Goupil Gallery in London; the reviews are adverse; only the Prince of Wales buys a canvas. He spends the summer in Arromanches and at the home of the Natansons. His second attack of delirium tremens in Paris; this time he believes he is being chased by the police. Fleury the publisher asks him to do the illustrations for the *Histoires Naturelles* by Jules Renard.

1899

A serious crisis of delirium tremens. Doctor Bourges, with the consent of the countess, commits him to the Madrid Clinic in Neuilly, run by Doctor Sénélaigue. The addiction cure seems to be effective. To prove that despite what the press says he is not mad, he paints the surprising series *The Circus* from memory, with the hope of gaining freedom. In *Le Figaro* Arsène Alexandre goes against the opinion of his colleagues and after a visit to Neuilly, writes that the state of the painter is "normal." After two months of commitment, he leaves the clinic and is put in the care of Paul Viaud, a friend of the family, who has to watch over him and stop him from drinking. He spends the summer in Normandy, where he starts to paint again, later he goes to Bordeaux, Arcachon and Malromé.

1900

He paints the scenery for the operetta *La Gitane* at the request of Thadée Natanson. He is a member of the jury for the section of posters in the International Exhibition. In June he rents a flat in Bordeaux, at number 66 Rue Caudéran, and a studio in Rue Porte-Dijeaux. He goes regularly to the Grand Theâtre and paints the actors of *La Belle Hélène* and *Messaline*. In Malromé, in December he suffers an attack of paralysis in both legs. He undergoes electric treatment, which is effective.

1901

He returns to Paris in April. In the Depeaux auction his canvases fetch considerable prices. He puts his studio in order before leaving for Taussat, on the banks of the Bassin du Arcachon where, on August 15, he suffers another attack of paralysis. His mother takes him to Malromé, where he dies on September 15 at the age of thirty-seven. He is given a Christian burial in Saint-André-du-Bois and later his corpse is taken to the cemetery of Verdelais.

SELECTED BIBLIOGRAPHY

ADRIANI, Götz. *Toulouse-Lautrec. The Complete Graphic Works*. London: Thames and Hudson, 1988.

ADHÉMAR, Jean. *Toulouse-Lautrec. Lithograpies. Pointes sèches. Œuvre complète*. Paris: Arts et Métiers Graphiques, 1965.

BOURET, Jean. *Toulouse-Lautrec*. Paris: Ed. Somogy, 1963.

CASTLEMAN, Riva and WITROCK, Wolfgang. *Henry de Toulouse-Lautrec. Images of the 1890s*. New York: The Museum of Modern Art, 1985.

COOPER, Douglas. *Henri de Toulouse-Lautrec*. New York: H.N. Abrams, 1982.

DELTEIL, Loys. *Le Peintre-Graveur Illustré*, Volumes X and XI, Paris, 1920.

DEVOISINS, Jean. *Catalogue Musée Toulouse-Lautrec*. Albi, no date.

FOCILLON, Henri. *Dessins de Toulouse-Lautrec*, Lausanne: Mermod, 1959.

HARRIS, Nathaniel. *El arte de Toulouse-Lautrec*. Barcelona: Ediciones Polígrafa, 1981.

HUISMAN, P.H. and DORTU, M.G. *Lautrec por Lautrec*. Barcelona: Blume, 1982.

JEDLICKA, Gotthard. *Henri de Toulouse-Lautrec*. Zurich: Rensch Verlag, 1943.

JOURDAIN, Francis and ADHÉMAR, Jean. *Toulouse-Lautrec*. Paris: Éditions Pierre Tisné, 1987.

JOYANT, Maurice. *Henri de Toulouse-Lautrec*, Volumes I and II, Paris: P. Floury, 1926-1927.

JULIEN, Edouard. *Les affiches de Toulouse-Lautrec*. Montecarlo: A. Sauret, 1951.

Dessins de Lautrec. Paris: Braun, 1951.

KELLER, Horts. *Toulouse-Lautrec*. Cologne: Du-Mont Schauberg Verlag, 1968.

LANDOLT, Hanspeter. *Henri Toulouse-Lautrec. Acquarelli, pastelli e disegni a colori*. Bérgamo: Institute Italiano d'Arti Grafiche, 1963.

LASSAIGNE, Jacques. *Toulouse-Lautrec*, Paris: Hyperion, 1939.

Lautrec, Geneva: Skira, 1953.

Toulouse-Lautrec et le Paris des Cabarets. Pully: Agence Internationale d'Édition, 1981.

LE TARGAT, François. *Toulouse-Lautrec*. Barcelona: Ediciones Polígrafa, 1988.

MAC ORLAND, Pierre. *Henri de Toulouse-Lautrec*, Paris: P. Floury, 1934.

NOVOTNY, Fritz. *Toulouse-Lautrec*. Paris: Éditions Cercle d'Art, 1970.

POLÁŠEK, Jan. *Toulouse-Lautrec. Dibujos*. Barcelona: Ediciones Polígrafa, 1980.

SCHMIDT, L. *Toulouse-Lautrec*. Paris: Imprimerie des Arts et Manufacture, 1987.

WITTROCK, Wolfgang. *Toulouse-Lautrec. The Complete Prints*. London: Sotheby's Publications, 1985 (2 vols.).

ILLUSTRATIONS

1. *Countess Adèle de Toulouse-Lautrec.* 1881.
   Oil on canvas, 36⅞ × 31⅞ in. (93.5 × 81 cm).
   Musée Toulouse-Lautrec, Albi.

1

2. *Count Alphonse de Toulouse-Lautrec*. 1881.
Oil on board, 9¼ × 5½ in. (23.5 × 14 cm).
Musée Toulouse-Lautrec, Albi.

3. *Countess Adèle de Toulouse-Lautrec*. 1882.
Oil on canvas, 16⅛ × 12¾ in. (41 × 32.5 cm).
Musée Toulouse-Lautrec, Albi.

4

4. *In the Harem*. 1882.
    Oil on board, 8⅝ × 6¼ in. (22 × 16 cm).
    Musée Toulouse-Lautrec, Albi.

5. *Study of a Nude*. 1882.
    Oil on board, 6½ × 9½ in. (16.5 × 24 cm).
    Musée Toulouse-Lautrec, Albi.

6. *Study of a Nude. Woman Sitting on a Divan*. 1882.
    Oil on canvas, 21⅝ × 18⅛ in. (55 × 46 cm).
    Musée Toulouse-Lautrec, Albi.

5

7

8

7. *Gin Cocktail.* 1886.
    Charcoal and chalk on paper, 18¾ × 24⅜ in. (47.5 × 62 cm).
    Musée Toulouse-Lautrec, Albi.

8. *Artilleryman and Girl.* 1886.
    Tracing with highlighted turpentine colors,
    22⅞ × 18⅛ in. (58 × 46 cm).
    Musée Toulouse-Lautrec, Albi.

9. *Artilleryman and Girl.* 1886.
    Oil on tracing paper, 22 × 17¾ in. (56 × 45 cm).
    Musée Toulouse-Lautrec, Albi.

10. *The Laundress.* 1885.
   Oil on board, 9½ × 6¾ in. (24 × 17 cm).
   Musée Toulouse-Lautrec, Albi.

11. *Ballet Scene.* 1886.
Oil on canvas, 40⅛ × 59⅞ in. (102 × 152 cm).
Thielska Galleriet, Stockholm.

11

12. *Juliette Vary.* 1887.
    Oil on cardboard, 13¾ × 7⅝ in. (35 × 19.5 cm).
    Musée Toulouse-Lautrec, Albi.

13. *Countess Adèle de Toulouse-Lautrec in the Salon of the Castle of Malromé*. 1887.
Oil on canvas, 23¼ × 21¼ in. (59 × 54 cm).
Musée Toulouse-Lautrec, Albi.

14. *In the Moulin de la Galette. La Goulue and Valentin le Désossé.* 1887.
Oil on cardboard, 20½ × 15⅜ in. (52 × 39 cm).
Musée Toulouse-Lautrec, Albi.

15. *In the Élysée Montmartre Dance-Hall.* 1887.
Paint on paper pasted onto canvas, 31⅞×25⅝ in. (81×65 cm).
Musée Toulouse-Lautrec, Albi.

16. *At the Circus Fernando: the Amazon.* 1888.
Oil on canvas, 39⅜×63⅜ in. (100×161 cm).
The Art Institute of Chicago.
Joseph Winterbotham Collection.

15

16

17

18

19

17. *View of the Bassin du Arcachon from the Yacht "Cocorico."* 1889.
   Oil on cardboard, 10⅝ × 14⅝ in. (27 × 37 cm).
   Musée Toulouse-Lautrec, Albi.

18. *The Drinker.* 1889.
   Ink, blue pencil and Conté pencil, 19¼ × 24¼ in. (49 × 63 cm).
   Musée Toulouse-Lautrec, Albi.

19. *In the Moulin de la Galette.* 1889.
   Oil on canvas, 34⅞ × 39¾ in. (88.5 × 101 cm).
   The Art Institute of Chicago.
   Mr. and Mrs. Lewis Larned Memorial Collection.

20. *Portrait of Henri Samary.* 1889.
   Oil on cardboard, 29½ × 20½ in. (75 × 52 cm).
   Musée d'Orsay, Paris.

20

21. *Désiré Dihau.* 1890.
     Oil on cardboard, 22 × 17¾ in. (56 × 45 cm).
     Musée Toulouse-Lautrec, Albi.

22. *Désiré Dihau, Bassoonist at the Opera.* 1890.
     Oil on board, 13¾ × 10⅝ in. (35 × 27 cm).
     Musée Toulouse-Lautrec, Albi.

23. *Mademoiselle Dihau at the Piano.* 1890.
     Oil on cardboard, 26¾ × 19⅛ in. (68 × 48.5 cm).
     Musée Toulouse-Lautrec, Albi.

21

22

24

25

26

24. *Gabrielle the Dancer*. 1890.
Oil on cardboard, 20⅞ × 15¾ in. (53 × 40 cm).
Musée Toulouse-Lautrec, Albi.

25. *Trapeze Artist (Adjusting her Leotard)*. 1890.
Oil on cardboard, 26¾ × 20½ in. (68 × 52 cm).
Musée Toulouse-Lautrec, Albi.

26. *In the Moulin Rouge: the Dance*. 1890.
Oil on canvas, 45¼ × 59 in. (115 × 150 cm).
Henry P. McIlhenny Collection, Philadelphia.

27. *The Woman with Gloves*. 1890.
Oil on cardboard, 21¼ × 15¾ in. (54 × 40 cm).
Musée d'Orsay, Paris.

27

28. *Redheaded Woman Seen from Behind.* 1891.
    Oil on cardboard, 30¾ × 23⅝ in. (78 × 60 cm).
    Musée Toulouse-Lautrec, Albi.

29. *Moulin Rouge. La Goulue and Valentin le Désossé.* 1891.
    Charcoal with color highlights, 60⅝ × 46½ in. (154 × 118 cm).
    Musée Toulouse-Lautrec, Albi.

30. *Moulin Rouge (La Goulue).* 1891.
    Poster, color lithograph, 76⅜ × 48 in. (194 × 122 cm).
    Musée Toulouse-Lautrec, Albi.

28

29

31

31. *The Two Friends*. 1891.
    Oil on cardboard, 18⅞ × 13⅜ in. (48 × 34 cm).
    Tate Gallery, London.

32. *«À la mie»*. 1891.
    Oil on cardboard, 20⅞ × 26¾ in. (53 × 68 cm).
    Museum of Fine Arts, Boston.

32

33. *In the Nouveau Cirque.* 1891.
    Watercolor, 45⅝ × 33⅛ in. (116 × 84 cm).
    Philadelphia Museum of Art, Philadelphia.
    Acquired by the John D. McIlhenny Fund.

34. *La Goulue Entering the Moulin Rouge.* 1891-1892.
Oil on cardboard, 31⅛ × 22⅞ in. (79.4 × 58 cm).
The Museum of Modern Art Collection, New York.
Donated by Mrs. David M. Levy.

35. *In the Moulin Rouge: Dancing a Waltz.* 1892.
Oil on cardboard, 32⅝ × 31½ in. (93 × 80 cm).
National Gallery, Prague.

36. *The Englishman in the Moulin Rouge.* 1892.
    Lithograph, 18½ × 14⅝ in. (47 × 37 cm).

Imp. Edw: Ancourt à Paris.

37. *In the Moulin Rouge: Portrait of Mr. Warner*. 1892.
    Oil on cardboard, 22½ × 17¾ in. (57 × 45 cm).
    Musée Toulouse-Lautrec, Albi.

38. *Ambassadeurs. Aristide Bruant and his Cabaret*. 1892.
    Brown paper and tracing paper on canvas, 100⅜ × 47¼ in. (255 × 120 cm).
    Musée Toulouse-Lautrec, Albi.

37

38

39. *The Hanged Man*. 1892.
 Poster, lithography, 30⅜ × 22 in. (77 × 56 cm).

40. *The Hanged Man*. 1892.
 Charcoal study for a poster, 26⅜ × 18⅞ in. (67 × 48 cm).
 Musée Toulouse-Lautrec, Albi.

41. *Ambassadeurs. Aristide Bruant*. 1892.
 Poster, color lithograph, 59 × 39⅜ in. (150 × 100 cm).

39

40

AMBASSADEURS...

aristide
BRUANT
dans
son cabaret

Hautrec

IMP. EDW ANCOURT & Cie 83 Fg St DENIS

42. *Study for the Poster "Reine de Joie."* 1892.
    Charcoal, 59⅞ × 41⅜ in. (152 × 105 cm).
    Musée Toulouse-Lautrec, Albi.

43. *At the Moulin Rouge.* 1892.
    Oil on cardboard, 48⅜ × 55⅜ in. (123 × 140.5 cm).
    The Art Institute of Chicago.
    Helen Birch Bartlett Memorial Collection.

44. *«Reine de Joie».* 1892.
    Poster, color lithograph, 53½ × 35⅞ in. (136 × 91 cm).

42

43

Reine de Joie
par
Victor Joze

chez
tous les
libraires

Imp. Edw. ANCOURT &Cᵉ PARIS

45. *Ballet de Papa Chrysanthème.* 1892.
   Oil on cardboard, 25⅝ × 22⅞ in. (65 × 58 cm).
   Musée Toulouse-Lautrec, Albi.

45

46. *Woman in Black Boa.* 1892.
 Oil on cardboard, 20½ × 16⅛ in. (52 × 41 cm).
 Musée d'Orsay, Paris.

47. *Jane Avril Leaving the Moulin Rouge*. 1892.
    Gouache on cardboard, 33¼×25 in. (84.5×63.5 cm).
    Wadsthworth Atheneum, Hartford, Connecticut.
    Legacy of George A. Gay.

48. *Jane Avril Entering the Moulin Rouge*. 1892.
    Oil on cardboard, 40⅛×21⅝ in. (102×55 cm).
    The Courtauld Institute of Art, London.

48

49. *Jardin de Paris. Jane Avril.* 1893.
    Poster, color lithograph, 51¼×37⅜ in. (130×95 cm).

50. *Divan Japonais.* 1893.
    Poster, color lithograph, 31½ × 23⅝ in. (80 × 60 cm).

51. *Naked Girl.* 1893.
    Oil on cardboard, 23⅜ × 15¾ in. (59.5 × 40 cm).
    Musée Toulouse-Lautrec, Albi.

52. *Loïe Fuller.* 1893.
    Lithograph hand-colored by Lautrec and powdered with gold metal
    paint, 14⅝ × 10¼ in. (37 × 26 cm).
    Musée Toulouse-Lautrec, Albi.

53. *Loïe Fuller in the Folies-Bergère.* 1893.
    Oil on cardboard, 24¾ × 17¾ in. (63 × 45 cm).
    Musée Toulouse-Lautrec, Albi.

52

51

54

55

54. *At La Renaissance:*
Sara Bernhardt in "Phaedra."
1893-1894.
Lithograph, 13⅜ × 9 in. (34 × 23 cm).
Musée Toulouse-Lautrec, Albi.

55. *At the Moulin Rouge:*
"Un rude, un vrai rude." 1893.
Lithograph,
18⅛ × 9⅝ in. (46 × 24.5 cm).
Musée Toulouse-Lautrec, Albi.

56. *The Box of the Golden Mask.* 1893.
Color lithography,
12 × 9½ in. (30.5 × 24 cm).
Musée Toulouse-Lautrec, Albi.

56

57. *The Box of the Golden Mask.* 1893.
Oil on canvas, 16⅛ × 12¾ in. (41 × 32.5 cm).
Musée Toulouse-Lautrec, Albi.

58. *Caudieux.* 1893.
   Poster, color lithograph, 51¼ × 37⅞ in. (130 × 95 cm).

59. *Aristide Bruant at his Cabaret.* 1893.
   Poster, color lithograph, 50 × 36⅜ in. (127 × 92.5 cm).

58

59

60. *"Le Matin": At the Foot of the Scaffold.* 1893.
    Poster, color lithograph, 33⅞ × 24⅜ in. (86 × 62 cm).

61. *Seated Woman.* 1893.
    Oil on cardboard, 22½ × 17⅜ in. (57 × 44 cm).
    Musée Toulouse-Lautrec, Albi.

62. *At the Gaieté Rochechouart: Nicolle.* 1893.
    Lithograph, 14 × 10½ in. (35.5 × 26.5 cm).
    Musée Toulouse-Lautrec, Albi

63. *The Gentleman, the Lady and the Dog.* 1893.
    Oil on canvas, 18⅞ × 23⅝ in. (48 × 60 cm).
    Musée Toulouse-Lautrec, Albi.

61

62

63

64. *The Card Game.* 1893.
Pastel, 22½ × 17⅜ in. (57 × 44 cm).
Hahnloser Collection, Bern.

65. *At the Top of the Stairs in Rue des Moulins. "Going up!" 1893.*
Oil on cardboard, 32½ × 23⅝ in. (82.5 × 60 cm).
Musée Toulouse-Lautrec, Albi.

66. *Louis Pascal.* 1893.
    Oil on cardboard, 31⅞ × 21¼ in. (81 × 54 cm).
    Musée Toulouse-Lautrec, Albi.

67. *Yvette Guilbert Greeting the Audience.* 1894.
Photographic proof of an original lithograph, highlighted with paint,
18⅜ × 11 in. (48 × 28 cm).
Musée Toulouse-Lautrec, Albi.

68. *Yvette Guilbert's Black Gloves.* 1894.
Oil on cardboard, 24¾ × 14⅝ in. (63 × 37 cm).
Musée Toulouse-Lautrec, Albi.

69. *Yvette Guilbert.* 1894.
Charcoal with touches of paint on brown paper,
73¼ × 36⅝ in. (186 × 93 cm).
Musée Toulouse-Lautrec, Albi.

67

68

70. *The Divan. Rolande.* 1894.
    Oil on cardboard, 20½ × 26⅜ in. (52 × 67 cm).
    Musée Toulouse-Lautrec, Albi.

71. *In the Salon of the Rue des Moulins.* 1894.
    Pastel, 43¾ × 52 in. (111 × 132 cm).
    Musée Toulouse-Lautrec, Albi.

70

71

72. *In the Salon of the Rue des Moulins.* 1894.
Oil on canvas, 43⅞ × 52⅛ in. (111.5 × 132.5 cm).
Musée Toulouse-Lautrec, Albi.

72

73. *La Goulue and Valentin.* 1894.
Lithograph, 11⅞ × 9 in. (30 × 23 cm).
Musée Toulouse-Lautrec, Albi.

74. «*Éros Vanné*». 1894.
Lithograph, 10⅞ × 7⅛ in. (27.5 × 18 cm).

75. *Leloir and Moreno in "The Wise Women."* 1894.
Lithograph, 14¾ × 10¼ in. (37.5 × 26 cm).
Musée Toulouse-Lautrec, Albi.

76. *L'Artisan Moderne.* 1894.
Poster, color lithograph, 35½ × 25 in. (90 × 63.5 cm).
Musée Toulouse-Lautrec, Albi.

73

74

75

78. *Confetti.* 1894.
   Poster; color lithograph, 21½ × 15¾ in. (54.5 × 40 cm).
   Musée Toulouse-Lautrec, Albi.

79

79. *Woman Lying with her Arms Upraised.* 1894.
Oil on cardboard, 18½ × 18½ in. (47 × 47 cm).
Musée Toulouse-Lautrec, Albi.

80. *Woman Pulling off her Stocking.* 1894.
Oil on cardboard, 24¼ × 17½ in. (61.5 × 44.5 cm).
Musée Toulouse-Lautrec, Albi.

80

81. *Woman Pulling on her Stocking.* 1894.
    Oil on cardboard, 22⅞ × 18⅛ in. (58 × 46 cm).
    Musée d'Orsay, Paris.

81

82. *The Two Friends.* 1894.
   Oil on cardboard, 18⅞ × 13⅝ in. (48 × 34.5 cm).
   Musée Toulouse-Lautrec, Albi.

83. *Doctor Tapié de Céleyran.* 1894.
   Oil on canvas, 43¼ × 22 in. (110 × 56 cm).
   Musée Toulouse-Lautrec, Albi.

84. *The Brothel Laundryman.* 1894.
    Oil on cardboard, 22⅞×18⅛ in. (58×46 cm).
    Musée Toulouse-Lautrec, Albi.

85. *At the Folies-Bergère. Three Figurants.* 1894.
    Oil on cardboard, 27⅛×23¼ in. (69×59 cm).
    Musée Toulouse-Lautrec, Albi.

86. *Woman in Gala Dress at the Entrance to a Theater Box.* 1894.
    Oil on canvas, 31⅞×20¼ in. (81×51.5 cm).
    Musée Toulouse-Lautrec, Albi.

84

85

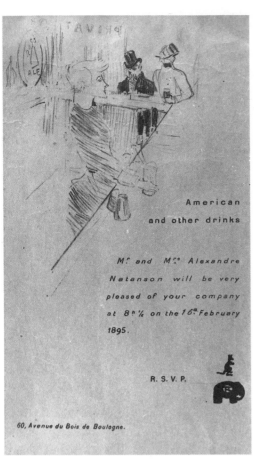

87.

87. *Alexandre Natanson Invitation.* 1895.
Lithograph, $10\frac{7}{8} \times 6\frac{1}{8}$ in. (27.5×15.5 cm).
Musée Toulouse-Lautrec, Albi.

88. *P. Sescau, Photographer.* 1894-1895.
Poster, color lithograph, $23\frac{5}{8} \times 31\frac{1}{2}$ in. (60×80 cm).
Musée Toulouse-Lautrec, Albi.

89. *Emilienne d'Alençon.* 1895.
Lithograph, $11\frac{5}{8} \times 9\frac{1}{2}$ in. (29.5×24 cm).
Musée Toulouse-Lautrec, Albi.

90. *Cléo de Mérode.* 1895.
Lithograph, $11\frac{5}{8} \times 9\frac{1}{2}$ in. (29.5×24 cm).
Musée Toulouse-Lautrec, Albi.

91. *La Troupe de Mlle. Églantine.* 1896.
Poster, color lithograph, $24\frac{1}{4} \times 31\frac{1}{2}$ in. (61.5×80 cm).

88

89

90

91

92. *La Goulue Dancing with Valentin le Désossé.* 1895.
Oil on canvas, 117⅜ × 124⅜ in. (298 × 316 cm).
Musée d'Orsay, Paris.

93. *The Moorish Dance or "Les Almées."* 1895.
Oil on canvas, 112¼ × 121¼ in. (285 × 308 cm).
Musée d'Orsay, Paris.

94. *Mademoiselle Polaire.* 1895.
    Oil on cardboard, 22 × 16⅛ in. (56 × 41 cm).
    Musée Toulouse-Lautrec, Albi.

94

95. *Madame Pascal at the Piano*. 1895.
    Oil on cardboard, 28 × 21½ in. (71 × 54.5 cm).
    Musée Toulouse-Lautrec, Albi.

96. *"La Chatelaine or Le Tocsin."* 1895.
  Poster, lithography, 22½ × 17¾ in. (57 × 45 cm).
  Musée Toulouse-Lautrec, Albi.

97. *Yvette Guilbert.* 1895.
  Ceramic, 20⅛ × 11 in. (51 × 28 cm).
  Musée Toulouse-Lautrec, Albi.

96

97

98. *Marcelle Lender Dancing the Bolero in "Chilpéric."* 1895.
Oil on canvas, 57⅛ × 59 in. (145 × 150 cm).
Mrs. John H. Whitney Collection, New York.

99. *The Clowness Cha-U-Kao*. 1895.
Oil on cardboard, 22½ × 16½ in. (57 × 42 cm).
Musée d'Orsay, Paris.

100. *The Clowness Cha-U-Kao*. 1895.
Oil on cardboard, 31⅛×23⅝ in. (81×60 cm).
Former Florence Gould Collection, New York.

101. *May Belfort.* 1895.
Poster, color lithograph, 31½ × 23⅝ in. (80 × 60 cm).
Musée Toulouse-Lautrec, Albi.

102. *La Revue Blanche.* 1895.
Charcoal with touches of color on paper, 58¼ × 41⅛ in.
(148 × 105 cm).
Musée Toulouse-Lautrec, Albi.

101

102

103. *La Revue Blanche.* 1895.
    Poster, color lithograph, 51¼×37⅞ in. (130×95 cm).

104. *May Milton.* 1895.
Poster, color lithograph, 30⅞ × 23⅝ in. (78.5 × 60 cm).

105. «*Skating: Professional Beauty*».
Mlle. Liane de Lancy in the Palais de Glace. 1896.
Oil on cardboard, 24⅜ × 19¼ in. (62 × 49 cm).
Musée Toulouse-Lautrec, Albi.

106. «*Skating: Professional Beauty*».
Mlle. Liane de Lancy in the Palais de Glace. 1896.
Paint and pencil on paper, 24⅜ × 18½ in. (62 × 47 cm).
Musée Toulouse-Lautrec, Albi.

107. *"L'Aube."* 1896.
Poster, lithography, 23⅝ × 31½ in. (60 × 80 cm).
Musée Toulouse-Lautrec, Albi.

105

106

107

108. *Figurant in a Review at the Folies-Bergère.* 1896.
Oil on cardboard, 28⅜ × 20¼ in. (72 × 51.5 cm).
Musée Toulouse-Lautrec, Albi.

109. *In the Wings. Folies-Bergère.* 1896.
India ink and blue pencil, 25⅝ × 19¾ in. (65 × 50 cm).
Musée Toulouse-Lautrec, Albi.

110. *The Great Concerts at the Opera. Ambroise Thomas at a Rehearsal of Françoise de Rimini.* 1896.
Paint, blue pencil and charcoal on brown paper,
31⅛ × 24 in. (79 × 61 cm).

108

109

110

111. *Maxime Dethomas at the Opera Dance.* 1896.
Gouache on cardboard, 26⅜ × 20½ in. (67 × 52 cm).
National Gallery of Art, Washington, D.C.
Chester Dale Collection.

112. *The Passenger on the No. 54.* 1896.
    Poster, color lithograph, 23¼ × 15 in. (59 × 38 cm).

113. *At the Concert.* 1896.
    Poster, color lithograph, 12⅝ × 9⅞ in. (32 × 25 cm).

112

113

114. *La Chaîne Simpson.* 1896.
  Poster, color lithograph, 34⅝ × 48⅞ in. (88 × 124 cm).
  Musée Toulouse-Lautrec, Albi.

114

115. *Chocolat Dancing.* 1896.
Paint, blue pencil and Conté pencil, 25⅝ × 19¾ in. (65 × 50 cm).
Musée Toulouse-Lautrec, Albi.

116. *The Awakening.* 1896.
Lithograph for «Elles», 15¾×20½ in. (40×52 cm).
Musée Toulouse-Lautrec, Albi.

117. «*The Chap Book*». 1896.
Poster, color lithograph, 16⅛×24 in. (41×61 cm).

116

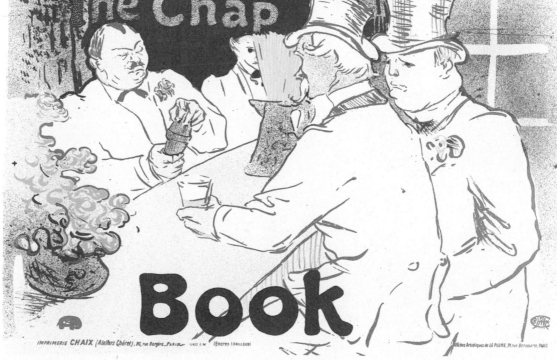

117

118. *La toilette.* 1896.
Oil on cardboard, 26⅜ × 21¼ in. (67 × 54 cm).
Musée d'Orsay, Paris.

119. *Women in a Brothel.* 1896.
Oil on cardboard, 23⅝ × 31½ in. (60 × 80 cm).
Beaux-Arts Museum, Budapest.

119

120. *«Alors, vous êtes sage?... Oui, madame, mais j'ai fréquenté quelqu'un!»*. Drawing published in "Le Rire", no. 114, 9 June 1897.
Paint and blue pencil, 28⅛ × 23¼ in. (71.5 × 59 cm).
Musée Toulouse-Lautrec, Albi.

121. *At the "Souris": Mme Palmyre and her Dog*. 1897.
Lead pencil on blued paper, 21⅝ × 14⅛ in. (55 × 36 cm).
Musée Toulouse-Lautrec, Albi.

120

121

122. *Elsa "The Viennese."* 1897.
Lithograph, 19⅛ × 14⅛ in. (48.5 × 36 cm).

123. *Madame Berthe Bady.* 1897.
Oil on cardboard, 27⅝ × 23⅝ in. (70 × 60 cm).
Musée Toulouse-Lautrec, Albi.

124. *In the Toilet.* 1898.
Oil on board, 24 × 19½ in. (61 × 49.5 cm).
Musée Toulouse-Lautrec, Albi.

125. *At the Bar: the Customer and the Anemic Cashier.* 1898.
Oil on cardboard, 31⅞×23⅝ in. (81×60 cm).
Kunsthaus, Zurich.

126. *The English Barmaid at the "Star" in Le Havre.* 1899.
Oil on board, 16⅛ × 12⅞ in. (41 × 32.8 cm).
Musée Toulouse-Lautrec, Albi.

128. *The Reticent One or "Au Rat Mort."* 1899.
Oil on board, 21⅝ × 18⅛ in. (55 × 46 cm).
The Courtauld Institute of Art, London.

129. *My Guardian. Madrid Sanatorium in Neuilly.* 1899.
Oil on board, 16⅞ × 14⅛ in. (43 × 36 cm).
Musée Toulouse-Lautrec, Albi.

130. *La Coutourière (Louise Blouet d'Enguin)*. 1900.
Oil on board, 24 × 19½ in. (61 × 49.5 cm).
Musée Toulouse-Lautrec, Albi.

131. *La Gitane. Théatre Antoine.* 1900.
Oil on cardboard, 31½ × 20⅞ in. (80 × 53 cm).
Musée Toulouse-Lautrec, Albi.

132. *Cocyte in "La Belle Héléne."* Bordeaux. 1900.
Watercolor, 24⅜ × 18⅞ in. (62 × 48 cm).
Musée Toulouse-Lautrec, Albi.

133. *In the Bordeaux Café.* 1900.
Pencil on paper, 18⅞ × 24⅜ in. (48 × 62 cm).
Musée Toulouse-Lautrec, Albi.

134. *La Gitane.* 1900.
Poster, color lithograph, 43⅛ × 25¼ in. (109.5 × 64 cm).
Musée Toulouse-Lautrec, Albi.

131

132

133

Théâtre
Antoine
La Gitane
de
Richepin

Imp. EUGÈNE VERNEAU, 108, Rue Folie Mèricourt. PARIS

135. *Maurice Joyant*. 1900.
Oil on board, 45⅞ × 31⅞ in. (116.5 × 81 cm).
Musée Toulouse-Lautrec, Albi.

136. *Carriage Being Pulled by a Cob*. 1900.
Oil on canvas, 24 × 19¾ in. (61 × 50 cm).
Musée Toulouse-Lautrec, Albi.

137. *Mesalina.* 1900.
Oil on canvas, 21⅝ × 18⅛ in. (55 × 46 cm).
Musée Toulouse-Lautrec, Albi.

138. *Mesalina Descending the Stairs, Flanked by Figurants.* 1900.
Oil on canvas, 39⅜ × 28¾ in. (100 × 73 cm).
Los Angeles County Museum.

139. *Paul Viaud as an Admiral.* 1901.
Oil on canvas, 54¾ × 60¼ in. (139 × 153 cm).
Museo de Arte de São Paulo, Brasil.

140. *An Examination in the Faculty of Medicine in the University of Paris.* 1901.
Oil on canvas, 25⅝ × 31⅞ in. (65 × 81 cm).
Musée Toulouse-Lautrec, Albi.

140

LIST OF ILLUSTRATIONS

126

41. *Ambassadeurs. Aristide Bruant.* 1892.
Poster, color lithograph,
59 × 39⅜ in. (150 × 100 cm).

42. *Study for the Poster "Reine de Joie."*
1892.
Charcoal,
59⅞ × 41⅜ in. (152 × 105 cm).
Musée Toulouse-Lautrec, Albi.

43. *At the Moulin Rouge.* 1892.
Oil on cardboard,
48⅜ × 55⅜ in. (123 × 140.5 cm).
The Art Institute of Chicago.
Helen Birch Bartlett Memorial
Collection.

44. *«Reine de Joie».* 1892.
Poster, color lithograph,
53½ × 35⅞ in. (136 × 91 cm).

45. *Ballet de Papa Chrysanthème.* 1892.
Oil on cardboard,
25⅝ × 22⅞ in. (65 × 58 cm).
Musée Toulouse-Lautrec, Albi.

46. *Woman in Black Boa.* 1892.
Oil on cardboard,
20½ × 16⅛ in. (52 × 41 cm).
Musée d'Orsay, Paris.

47. *Jane Avril Leaving the Moulin Rouge.*
1892.
Gouache on cardboard,
33¼ × 25 in. (84.5 × 63.5 cm).
Wadsthworth Atheneum, Hartford,
Connecticut.
Legacy of George A. Gay.

48. *Jane Avril Entering the Moulin Rouge.*
1892.
Oil on cardboard,
40⅛ × 21⅝ in. (102 × 55 cm).
The Courtauld Institute of Art,
London.

49. *Jardin de Paris. Jane Avril.* 1893.
Poster, color lithograph,
51¼ × 37⅜ in. (130 × 95 cm).

50. *Divan Japonais.* 1893.
Poster, color lithograph,
31½ × 23⅝ in. (80 × 60 cm).

51. *Naked Girl.* 1893.
Oil on cardboard,
23⅜ × 15¾ in. (59.5 × 40 cm).
Musée Toulouse-Lautrec, Albi.

52. *Loïe Fuller.* 1893.
Lithograph hand-colored by Lautrec
and powdered with gold metal paint,
14⅝ × 10¼ in. (37 × 26 cm).
Musée Toulouse-Lautrec, Albi.

53. *Loïe Fuller in the Folies-Bergère.* 1893.
Oil on cardboard,
24¾ × 17¾ in. (63 × 45 cm).
Musée Toulouse-Lautrec, Albi.

54. *At La Renaissance:*
Sara Bernhardt in "Phaedra."
1893-1894.
Lithograph,
13⅜ × 9 in. (34 × 23 cm).
Musée Toulouse-Lautrec, Albi.

55. *At the Moulin Rouge:*
"Un rude, un vrai rude." 1893.
Lithograph,
18⅛ × 9⅝ in. (46 × 24.5 cm).
Musée Toulouse-Lautrec, Albi.

56. *The Box of the Golden Mask.* 1893.
Color lithography,
12 × 9½ in. (30.5 × 24 cm).
Musée Toulouse-Lautrec, Albi.

57. *The Box of the Golden Mask.* 1893.
Oil on canvas,
16⅛ × 12¾ in. (41 × 32.5 cm).
Musée Toulouse-Lautrec, Albi.

58. *Caudieux.* 1893.
Poster, color lithograph,
51¼ × 37⅞ in. (130 × 95 cm).

59. *Aristide Bruant at his Cabaret.* 1893.
Poster, color lithograph,
50 × 36⅜ in. (127 × 92.5 cm).

60. *"Le Matin": At the Foot of the*
Scaffold. 1893.
Poster, color lithograph,
33⅞ × 24⅜ in. (86 × 62 cm).

61. *Seated Woman.* 1893.
Oil on cardboard,
22½ × 17⅜ in. (57 × 44 cm).
Musée Toulouse-Lautrec, Albi.

62. *At the Gaieté Rochechouart: Nicolle.*
1893.
Lithograph,
14 × 10½ in. (35.5 × 26.5 cm).
Musée Toulouse-Lautrec, Albi.

63. *The Gentleman, the Lady and the Dog.*
1893.
Oil on canvas,
18⅞ × 23⅝ in. (48 × 60 cm).
Musée Toulouse-Lautrec, Albi.

64. *The Card Game.* 1893.
Pastel,
22½ × 17⅜ in. (57 × 44 cm).
Hahnloser Collection, Bern.

65. *At the Top of the Stairs in Rue des*
Moulins. "Going up!" 1893.
Oil on cardboard,
32½ × 23⅝ in. (82.5 × 60 cm).
Musée Toulouse-Lautrec, Albi.

66. *Louis Pascal.* 1893.
Oil on cardboard,
31⅞ × 21¼ in. (81 × 54 cm).
Musée Toulouse-Lautrec, Albi.

67. *Yvette Guilbert Greeting the Audience.*
1894.
Photographic proof of an original
lithograph, highlighted with paint,
18⅜ × 11 in. (48 × 28 cm).
Musée Toulouse-Lautrec, Albi.

68. *Yvette Guilbert's Black Gloves.* 1894.
Oil on cardboard,
24¾ × 14⅝ in. (63 × 37 cm).
Musée Toulouse-Lautrec, Albi.

69. *Yvette Guilbert.* 1894.
Charcoal with touches of paint on
brown paper,
73¼ × 36⅝ in. (186 × 93 cm).
Musée Toulouse-Lautrec, Albi.

70. *The Divan. Rolande.* 1894.
Oil on cardboard,
20½ × 26⅜ in. (52 × 67 cm).
Musée Toulouse-Lautrec, Albi.

71. *In the Salon of the Rue des Moulins.*
1894.
Pastel,
43¾ × 52 in. (111 × 132 cm).
Musée Toulouse-Lautrec, Albi.

72. *In the Salon of the Rue des Moulins.*
1894.
Oil on canvas,
43⅞ × 52⅛ in. (111.5 × 132.5 cm).
Musée Toulouse-Lautrec, Albi.

73. *La Goulue and Valentin.* 1894.
Lithograph,
11⅞ × 9 in. (30 × 23 cm).
Musée Toulouse-Lautrec, Albi.

74. *«Éros Vanné».* 1894.
Lithograph,
10⅞ × 7⅛ in. (27.5 × 18 cm).

75. *Leloir and Moreno in "The Wise*
Women." 1894.
Lithograph,
14¾ × 10¼ in. (37.5 × 26 cm).
Musée Toulouse-Lautrec, Albi.

76. *L'Artisan Moderne.* 1894.
Poster, color lithograph, 35½ × 25 in.
(90 × 63.5 cm).
Musée Toulouse-Lautrec, Albi.

77. *Babylone d'Allemagne.* 1894.
Poster, color lithograph,
51¼ × 37⅜ in. (130 × 95 cm).

78. *Confetti.* 1894.
Poster, color lithograph,
21½ × 15¾ in. (54.5 × 40 cm).
Musée Toulouse-Lautrec, Albi.

79. *Woman Lying with her Arms Upraised.*
1894.
Oil on cardboard,
18½ × 18½ in. (47 × 47 cm).
Musée Toulouse-Lautrec, Albi.

80. *Woman Pulling off her Stocking.* 1894.
Oil on cardboard,
24¼ × 17½ in. (61.5 × 44.5 cm).
Musée Toulouse-Lautrec, Albi.

81. *Woman Pulling on her Stocking.* 1894.
Oil on cardboard,
22⅞ × 18⅛ in. (58 × 46 cm).
Musée d'Orsay, Paris.

82. *The Two Friends.* 1894.
Oil on cardboard,
18⅞ × 13⅝ in. (48 × 34.5 cm).
Musée Toulouse-Lautrec, Albi.

83. *Doctor Tapié de Céleyran.* 1894.
Oil on canvas,
43¼ × 22 in. (110 × 56 cm).
Musée Toulouse-Lautrec, Albi.

84. *The Brothel Laundryman.* 1894.
Oil on cardboard,
22⅞ × 18⅛ in. (58 × 46 cm).
Musée Toulouse-Lautrec, Albi.

85. *At the Folies-Bergère. Three Figurants.*
1894.
Oil on cardboard,
27⅛ × 23¼ in. (69 × 59 cm).
Musée Toulouse-Lautrec, Albi.

86. *Woman in Gala Dress at the Entrance*
to a Theater Box. 1894.
Oil on canvas,
31⅞ × 20¼ in. (81 × 51.5 cm).
Musée Toulouse-Lautrec, Albi.

87. *Alexandre Natanson Invitation.* 1895.
Lithograph,
10⅞ × 6⅛ in. (27.5 × 15.5 cm).
Musée Toulouse-Lautrec, Albi.

88. *P. Sescau, Photographer.* 1894-1895.
Poster, color lithograph,
23⅝ × 31½ in. (60 × 80 cm).
Musée Toulouse-Lautrec, Albi.

89. *Emilienne d'Alençon.* 1895.
Lithograph,
11⅝ × 9½ in. (29.5 × 24 cm).
Musée Toulouse-Lautrec, Albi.

90. *Cléo de Mérode.* 1895.
Lithograph,
11⅝ × 9½ in. (29.5 × 24 cm).
Musée Toulouse-Lautrec, Albi.

91. *La Troupe de Mlle. Églantine.* 1896.
Poster, color lithograph,
24¼ × 31½ in. (61.5 × 80 cm).

92. *La Goulue Dancing with Valentin le Désossé.* 1895.
Oil on canvas,
117⅜ × 124⅜ in. (298 × 316 cm).
Musée d'Orsay, Paris.

93. *The Moorish Dance or "Les Almées."* 1895.
Oil on canvas,
112¼ × 121¼ in. (285 × 308 cm).
Musée d'Orsay, Paris.

94. *Mademoiselle Polaire.* 1895.
Oil on cardboard,
22 × 16⅛ in. (56 × 41 cm).
Musée Toulouse-Lautrec, Albi.

95. *Madame Pascal at the Piano.* 1895.
Oil on cardboard,
28 × 21½ in. (71 × 54.5 cm).
Musée Toulouse-Lautrec, Albi.

96. *"La Chatelaine or Le Tocsin."* 1895.
Poster, lithography,
22½ × 17¾ in. (57 × 45 cm).
Musée Toulouse-Lautrec, Albi.

97. *Yvette Guilbert.* 1895.
Ceramic,
20⅛ × 11 in. (51 × 28 cm).
Musée Toulouse-Lautrec, Albi.

98. *Marcelle Lender Dancing the Bolero in "Chilpéric."* 1895.
Oil on canvas,
57⅛ × 59 in. (145 × 150 cm).
Mrs. John H. Whitney Collection, New York.

99. *The Clowness Cha-U-Kao.* 1895.
Oil on cardboard,
22½ × 16½ in. (57 × 42 cm).
Musée d'Orsay, Paris.

100. *The Clowness Cha-U-Kao.* 1895.
Oil on cardboard,
31⅞ × 23⅝ in. (81 × 60 cm).
Former Florence Gould Collection, New York.

101. *May Belfort.* 1895.
Poster, color lithograph,
31½ × 23⅝ in. (80 × 60 cm).
Musée Toulouse-Lautrec, Albi.

102. *La Revue Blanche.* 1895.
Charcoal with touches of color on paper,
58¼ × 41⅛ in. (148 × 105 cm).
Musée Toulouse-Lautrec, Albi.

103. *La Revue Blanche.* 1895.
Poster, color lithograph,
51¼ × 37⅞ in. (130 × 95 cm).

104. *May Milton.* 1895.
Poster, color lithograph,
30⅞ × 23⅝ in. (78.5 × 60 cm).

105. *«Skating: Professional Beauty». Mlle. Liane de Lancy in the Palais de Glace.* 1896.
Oil on cardboard,
24⅜ × 19¼ in. (62 × 49 cm).
Musée Toulouse-Lautrec, Albi.

106. *«Skating: Professional Beauty». Mlle. Liane de Lancy in the Palais de Glace.* 1896.
Paint and pencil on paper,
24⅜ × 18½ in. (62 × 47 cm).
Musée Toulouse-Lautrec, Albi.

107. *"L'Aube."* 1896.
Poster, lithography,
23⅝ × 31½ in. (60 × 80 cm).
Musée Toulouse-Lautrec, Albi.

108. *Figurant in a Review at the Folies-Bergère.* 1896.
Oil on cardboard,
28⅜ × 20¼ in. (72 × 51.5 cm).
Musée Toulouse-Lautrec, Albi.

109. *In the Wings. Folies-Bergère.* 1896.
India ink and blue pencil,
25⅝ × 19¾ in. (65 × 50 cm).
Musée Toulouse-Lautrec, Albi.

110. *The Great Concerts at the Opera. Ambroise Thomas at a Rehearsal of Françoise de Rimini.* 1896.
Paint, blue pencil and charcoal on brown paper,
31⅛ × 24 in. (79 × 61 cm).

111. *Maxime Dethomas at the Opera Dance.* 1896.
Gouache on cardboard,
26⅜ × 20½ in. (67 × 52 cm).
National Gallery of Art, Washington, D.C. Chester Dale Collection.

112. *The Passenger on the No. 54.* 1896.
Poster, color lithograph,
23¼ × 15 in. (59 × 38 cm).

113. *At the Concert.* 1896.
Poster, color lithograph,
12⅝ × 9⅞ in. (32 × 25 cm).

114. *La Chaîne Simpson.* 1896.
Poster, color lithograph,
34⅝ × 48⅞ in. (88 × 124 cm).
Musée Toulouse-Lautrec, Albi.

115. *Chocolat Dancing.* 1896.
Paint, blue pencil and Conté pencil,
25⅝ × 19¾ in. (65 × 50 cm).
Musée Toulouse-Lautrec, Albi.

116. *The Awakening.* 1896.
Lithograph for «Elles»,
15¾ × 20½ in. (40 × 52 cm).
Musée Toulouse-Lautrec, Albi.

117. *«The Chap Book».* 1896.
Poster, color lithograph,
16⅛ × 24 in. (41 × 61 cm).

118. *La toilette.* 1896.
Oil on cardboard,
26⅜ × 21¼ in. (67 × 54 cm).
Musée d'Orsay, Paris.

119. *Women in a Brothel.* 1896.
Oil on cardboard,
23⅝ × 31½ in. (60 × 80 cm).
Beaux-Arts Museum, Budapest.

120. *«Alors, vous êtes sage?... Oui, madame, mais j'ai fréquenté quelqu'un!».* Drawing published in "Le Rire", no. 114, 9 June 1897.
Paint and blue pencil,
28⅛ × 23¼ in. (71.5 × 59 cm).
Musée Toulouse-Lautrec, Albi.

121. *At the "Souris": Mme Palmyre and her Dog.* 1897.
Lead pencil on blued paper,
21⅝ × 14⅛ in. (55 × 36 cm).
Musée Toulouse-Lautrec, Albi.

122. *Elsa "The Viennese."* 1897.
Lithograph,
19⅛ × 14⅛ in. (48.5 × 36 cm).

123. *Madame Berthe Bady.* 1897.
Oil on cardboard,
27⅝ × 23⅝ in. (70 × 60 cm).
Musée Toulouse-Lautrec, Albi.

124. *In the Toilet.* 1898.
Oil on board,
24 × 19½ in. (61 × 49.5 cm).
Musée Toulouse-Lautrec, Albi.

125. *At the Bar: the Customer and the Anemic Cashier.* 1898.
Oil on cardboard,
31⅞ × 23⅝ in. (81 × 60 cm).
Kunsthaus, Zurich.

126. *The English Barmaid at the "Star" in Le Havre.* 1899.
Oil on board,
16⅛ × 12⅞ in. (41 × 32.8 cm).
Musée Toulouse-Lautrec, Albi.

127. *Jane Avril.* 1899.
Poster, color lithograph,
22 × 14⅛ in. (56 × 36 cm).
Musée Toulouse-Lautrec, Albi.

128. *The Reticent One or "Au Rat Mort."* 1899.
Oil on board,
21⅝ × 18⅛ in. (55 × 46 cm).
The Courtauld Institute of Art, London.

129. *My Guardian. Madrid Sanatorium in Neuilly.* 1899.
Oil on board,
16⅞ × 14⅛ in. (43 × 36 cm).
Musée Toulouse-Lautrec, Albi.

130. *La Coutourière (Louise Blouet d'Enguin).* 1900.
Oil on board,
24 × 19½ in. (61 × 49.5 cm).
Musée Toulouse-Lautrec, Albi.

131. *La Gitane. Théatre Antoine.* 1900.
Oil on cardboard,
31½ × 20⅞ in. (80 × 53 cm).
Musée Toulouse-Lautrec, Albi.

132. *Cocyte in "La Belle Héléne." Bordeaux.* 1900.
Watercolor,
24⅜ × 18⅞ in. (62 × 48 cm).
Musée Toulouse-Lautrec, Albi.

133. *In the Bordeaux Café.* 1900.
Pencil on paper,
18⅞ × 24⅜ in. (48 × 62 cm).
Musée Toulouse-Lautrec, Albi.

134. *La Gitane.* 1900.
Poster, color lithograph,
43⅛ × 25¼ in. (109.5 × 64 cm).
Musée Toulouse-Lautrec, Albi.

135. *Maurice Joyant.* 1900.
Oil on board,
45⅞ × 31⅞ in. (116.5 × 81 cm).
Musée Toulouse-Lautrec, Albi.

136. *Carriage Being Pulled by a Cob.* 1900.
Oil on canvas,
24 × 19¾ in. (61 × 50 cm).
Musée Toulouse-Lautrec, Albi.

137. *Mesalina.* 1900.
Oil on canvas,
21⅝ × 18⅛ in. (55 × 46 cm).
Musée Toulouse-Lautrec, Albi.

138. *Mesalina Descending the Stairs, Flanked by Figurants.* 1900.
Oil on canvas,
39⅜ × 28¾ in. (100 × 73 cm).
Los Angeles County Museum.

139. *Paul Viaud as an Admiral.* 1901.
Oil on canvas,
54¾ × 60¼ in. (139 × 153 cm).
Museo de Arte de São Paulo, Brasil.

140. *An Examination in the Faculty of Medicine in the University of Paris.* 1901.
Oil on canvas,
25⅝ × 31⅞ in. (65 × 81 cm).
Musée Toulouse-Lautrec, Albi.